The Stars Speak

THE STARS SPEAK

Tankas on the Mazzaroth

Stephanie Mathews

RESOURCE *Publications* · Eugene, Oregon

THE STARS SPEAK
Tankas on the Mazzaroth

Copyright © 2022 Stephanie Mathews. All rights reserved. Except for brief quotations in critical publications or reviews, no part of this book may be reproduced in any manner without prior written permission from the publisher. Write: Permissions, Wipf and Stock Publishers, 199 W. 8th Ave., Suite 3, Eugene, OR 97401.

Resource Publications
An Imprint of Wipf and Stock Publishers
199 W. 8th Ave., Suite 3
Eugene, OR 97401

www.wipfandstock.com

PAPERBACK ISBN: 978-1-6667-5858-0
HARDCOVER ISBN: 978-1-6667-5859-7
EBOOK ISBN: 978-1-6667-5860-3

11/11/22

Scripture taken from the New King James Version®. Copyright © 1982 by Thomas Nelson. Used by permission. All rights

Contents

Introduction	ix

PROLOGUE: THE BEGINNING
The Zodiac	3

CHAPTER ONE: VIRGO
The Virgin	7
The Desired	8
The Centaur	9
The Coming One	10

CHAPTER TWO: LIBRA
The Scales	13
The Southern Cross	14
The Victim	15
The Crown	16

CHAPTER THREE: SCORPIO
The Scorpion	19
The Serpent Holder	20
The Serpent	21
The Mighty One	22

Chapter Four: Sagittarius
- The Archer — 25
- The Harp — 26
- The Altar — 27
- The Dragon — 28

Chapter Five: Capricorn
- The Goat — 31
- The Arrow — 32
- The Eagle — 33
- The Dolphin — 34

Chapter Six: Aquarius
- The Water-Pourer — 37
- The Southern Fish — 38
- The Winged Horse — 39
- The Swan — 40

Chapter Seven: Pisces
- The Fishes — 43
- The Bands — 44
- The Chained Woman — 45
- The Crowned King — 46

Chapter Eight: Aries
- The Ram — 49
- The Enthroned Woman — 50
- The Sea-Monster — 51
- The Breaker — 52

Chapter Nine: Taurus
- The Bull — 55
- The Glorious One — 56
- The River — 57
- The Shepherd — 58

Chapter Ten: Gemini
- The Twins — 61
- The Enemy — 62
- The Prince — 63
- The Redeemer — 64

Chapter Eleven: Cancer
- The Crab — 67
- The Lesser Sheepfold — 68
- The Greater Sheepfold — 69
- The Ship — 70

Chapter Twelve: Leo
- The Lion — 73
- The Serpent — 74
- The Cup — 75
- The Raven — 76

Epilogue: The Ending
- The Mazzaroth — 79

Introduction

The word Mazzaroth means constellations. The book of Job chapter 38 verse 32 reads, *"Can you bring out Mazzaroth in its season? Or can you guide the Great Bear with its cubs?"*

Long before people had the Bible written in its entirety, God revealed His plan of salvation in the stars. As with many things, the story of the constellations became corrupted and its meaning distorted.

The following book of tankas tell the story of the Mazzaroth. Each zodiac sign and its three decans make up a chapter and show the story of redemption through Jesus Christ.

Prologue
The Beginning

The Zodiac

Look up in the sky
The Mazzaroth you will see
It tells the story
Of the One who can redeem
All from the bondage of death

Chapter One
Virgo

The Virgin

Start with the maiden
You will see the beginning
Of this great story
The maiden is the mother
From her seed The Branch will come

The Desired

The desired Son
Sits upon the maiden's lap
She will be called blessed
A virgin to carry Him
The One who nations long for

The Centaur

Fully God and Man
Yet He came down born of flesh
To heal and save
A sacrifice was needed
He willingly gave His life

The Coming One

The Pierced One will come
To conquer and separate
The sheep from the goats
As foretold, He will return
To judge the world as The King

Chapter Two
Libra

The Scales

The scales weighing
Redemption comes at a cost
Death is the payment
The balance is negative
Jesus Christ has paid the debt

The Southern Cross

The cross is the hope
In not separating us
From our Creator
Jesus cut off for the sins
For all our iniquities

The Victim

A lamb to be slain
The Lamb of God offered up
Voluntary death
Bloodshed for the forgiveness
Sins punished and washed away

The Crown

The Victor was here
The One who overcame death
He is King of all
He died and rose from the grave
His reign is over all things

Chapter Three
Scorpio

The Scorpion

Death carries a sting
Conflicts and wars follow us
The devil brings it
His hate is overflowing
The sting of his words deceive

The Serpent Holder

The serpent looks up
He sees the crown of glory
He desires it
The Serpent Holder subdues
He is King and Conqueror

The Serpent

The antagonist
The serpent attacks again
He wants to be God
He doesn't have the power
All power belongs to God

The Mighty One

The Mighty One comes
El Gibbor comes to save all
To destroy evil
Our Savior has come to us
His return will bring justice

Chapter Four
Sagittarius

The Archer

The Centaur is here
Fully man and fully God
Coming to destroy
The victory will be His
Satan cast into the pit

The Harp

Sing praises to Him
His followers can rejoice
He is exalted
Make a joyful noise to Him
The glory belongs to Him

The Altar

A fire prepared
His enemies shall go down
His wrath will engulf
Vengeance belongs to the Lord
The wicked will not escape

The Dragon

A dragon cast out
He deceived the whole world
In believing lies
The devil disguised as light
But he will be trodden down

Chapter Five
Capricorn

The Goat

Spotless sacrifice
Required for atonement
The blood must be shed
To wash away transgressions
Follow and be born again

The Arrow

An arrow to kill
The iniquity of all
God's wrath will be known
The standard cannot be changed
Judgment can't be avoided

The Eagle

A wounded Eagle
A glorious bird flying
Wings spread over us
Feeding us with His body
His blood is all that saves us

The Dolphin

Plunged down to Hades
Punished by God for our sin
Yet He conquered death
Rising from the depths of hell
Leaping out of the darkness

Chapter Six
Aquarius

The Water-Pourer

Let all who thirst come
New life to be found in Him
The Spirit poured out
We must live in God's Spirit
Keeping in stride with our Lord

The Southern Fish

We have been transformed
A new creature has been born
Escaping the death
By the power of the Lord
The Living Water poured out

The Winged Horse

A Messenger comes
Flying high for all to see
The Word has come forth
The Spirit empowering
Flying in heaven and earth

The Swan

A beautiful cross
A crucifixion was done
The Glorious One
But death was not strong enough
The final victory won

Chapter Seven

Pisces

The Fishes

Two tied together
United under the One
To cast out the net
And become fishers of men
Proclaiming the truth to all

The Bands

We are in bondage
The enemy wounded us
Caught up in ourselves
But there is a Redeemer
Who will bind our hearts to Him

The Chained Woman

Bride of Jesus Christ
The weak, afflicted, and chained
A Rescuer comes
To break the enemies hold
He rules and we reign with Him

The Crowned King

The King on His throne
Risen and Ruler of all
The One to rule
The Lamb that was slain rose up
The Lion is the True King

Chapter Eight
Aries

The Ram

Worthy is the One
The Lamb of God came to us
He came to bring life
The bride of the Lamb rejoice
He holds all life in His hands

The Enthroned Woman

We are to be raised
His bride waiting His return
A marriage to come
At last rejoicing with Him
In eternity with Him

The Sea-Monster

The evil looms large
Engulfing the world in lies
God seems to be gone
But He binds the enemy
The Strong One will over throw

The Breaker

The Breaker has come
The Son of the Most Divine
Persecution comes
The Son is victorious
He will carry us away

Chapter Nine
Taurus

The Bull

Judgment is coming
The Lamb returning to judge
His glory shining
His wrath and fury unleashed
His enemies in the pit

The Glorious One

The Brilliant One shines
He is the Strong One coming
Hunting the devil
He will slay the enemy
Swiftly destroying evil

The River

River of the Judge
A fiery river flows
The books are opened
Like fire is His judgment
Engulfing His enemies

The Shepherd

The Chief Shepherd comes
To gather His flock to Him
He will carry them
Wrath for all who won't believe
The flock safe with Auriga

Chapter Ten
Gemini

The Twins

United with Christ
His mission a twofold plan
He came to suffer
He will return to conquer
And reign forever supreme

The Enemy

The evil one comes
To devour all in sight
He comes to deceive
But he will be bound with chains
And cast down into the pit

The Prince

Sirius is Prince
The Prince of Peace came to us
Prince to all the earth
He will be revealed to all
The Sent Prince coming to judge

The Redeemer

He's the Redeemer
Who came to bring redemption
The burden on Him
To redeem us to our God
To carry us to heaven

Chapter Eleven
Cancer

The Crab

Consider the end
The end of the life you know
He brings completion
The redeemed will be kept safe
In the possession of Christ

The Lesser Sheepfold

Herd of animals
The gathering of His flock
The Pole Star is here
Giving direction to see
As we wait for His return

The Greater Sheepfold

The assembly
The purchased gathered to Him
A Rescuer came
Protected from second death
The book of life kept by God

The Ship

The ship is at rest
In a safe harbor at home
Our captain is Christ
He is the Ark of safety
He saves all who come to Him

Chapter Twelve
Leo

The Lion

The Lion to come
The King of Kings is coming
To tear asunder
The Lion will prevail
He will be victorious

The Serpent

Lucifer cast down
The angel of light now dark
Satan is trampled
For his deception
His followers go down too

The Cup

The cup of wrath poured
Fire and brimstone coming
The wicked consumed
Enemies will be destroyed
The rebellious are punished

The Raven

Final destruction
A battle at the end times
The Raven will tear
Those that rebelled and followed
The deceiver's lies and ways

Epilogue
The Ending

The Mazzaroth

God has always shown
How the world begins and ends
He sent a Savior
To save from the second death
Heaven declares His Glory

www.ingramcontent.com/pod-product-compliance
Lightning Source LLC
Chambersburg PA
CBHW071733040426
42446CB00012B/2340